EPIPHANY

EPIPHANY

A collection of Life quotes and proverbs

E. J. MAMHOT

Epiphany

Copyright © 2020 by Erwin John Mamhot. All rights reserved.

No part of this publication may be reproduced, stored in a retrieval system or transmitted in any way by any means, electronic, mechanical, photocopy, recording or otherwise without the prior permission of the author except as provided by USA copyright law.

Front cover design by Jim Villaflores.
jimville.designs@gmail.com

Book interior design by Joseph Apuhin.

Published in the United States of America

ISBN 978-1-64753-178-2 (Paperback)

31.01.20

This book is dedicated to my partner, Catherine, my Mom, Naomi, my niece, Aubree, my siblings, Sherna, Jayr, Chris, and to my late Dad in heaven, Sherwin.

There are reasons that the heart knows but the mind knows nothing of.

If you work 8 hours a day, give your all within that 8 hours, but never do overtime. 8 hours is enough time for work. Spend the rest of the day with your family, your partner, or your friends.

It only takes a few seconds to say such beautiful 3 words. If these words are genuine, spend a lifetime to prove it.

When you fall in love, give your 100%.

People change and their priorities change. Do not hold any grudges about the past.

Do not stress yourself trying to control the people around you, the only person you can control is yourself.

If you're thinking of doing something, do it today. Do not wait for tomorrow.

Family is EVERYTHING.

As much as possible speak of KIND words only.

Do not be too possessive over someone or something.

Never forget the Magic words such as I'm Sorry, I love you, Thank you, You're welcome.

Everyday is an opportunity to learn from everything around us. Learning is just optional.

Family is not an Option, they should be our priority.

True Love can change everything about you.

Once you are in a relationship, do not fall for other people with Infatuation and Lust. Chances are, you can never go back to the person you fell in love with.

Everyone wants Honesty when in fact no one is really Honest.

Life is Hard but Life is harder for some people. Let us make Life easier for everyone.

Help as much as you can. Give as much as you can. You'll never know you might need some help too someday.

Always remember. Kindness begets Kindness.

Everyone wants good Health, but most of us have been living an unhealthy life our whole lives, mentally and physically.

Let go of Hate, either to your friends, family, or your partner, Hate will do you no good.

For most, Hating is so easy, but Forgiving is just so hard.

True beauty cannot be seen on the outside. Do not be deceived.

In a relationship, the woman is always right. You cannot argue with that.

The Lord works in mysterious ways.

Never judge anyone by their appearance.

Travel while you're still young. You'll surely want to do that when you're older but won't have enough energy to do it.

Long distance relationships won't work for most.

The eyes never lie.

Don't live in Fear.

Never question your Faith in God.

Food is more addictive than drugs.

Pushing yourself to the limit could either make you stronger or break you down.

Just like what they all say; Laughter is the best medicine.

Do not throw rude words to anyone over anger. Your anger may move on, but the person you've thrown those words into may not.

For some people, they've learned more from the streets than in any classroom.

Life is better if you're sober. Being wasted is such a waste of life.

Money can buy temporary happiness. Permanent happiness is something money can't buy.

Never use anyone as your emotional punching bag, most especially your partner or any of your family member.

For most 100 years in this lifetime is not possible, but you can live this life with 100% of yourself.

Never brag about what you have. We're all just passing through, you'll eventually lose everything one day. Stay humble.

You won't get wrong by choosing the right decisions.

At the end of the day, we always choose what makes us happy anyway, just follow what your heart desires.

If you are too sensitive, do not ask for advice if you do not want to get offended.

Love your Mom and Dad, by the time they are gone you'll never have another one.

Give time to exercise while you're young, you'll realize the importance of it once you're older.

If you're frustrated, in pain, confused, stressed or pressured. Pray and read the Bible. It will give you peace of mind.

Never forget to give thanks and praise to the Lord.

There is Hope when There is Life.

Respect begets Respect.

Most of us believe in our own lies.

Riding a motorcycle in an open road is a type of freedom a non-rider would never understand.

Being successful is never a race, just ride this life with your own pace. As long as you've experienced happiness with your journey to success, that's what matters most.

Being promiscuous or polygamous is never a good practice, it only gives you false happiness.

By the time you find contentment in life, you will find genuine happiness.

If you're tired, then Rest, but don't you ever quit.

Do not buy a lot of things that you want, chances are you might sell the things that you need one day.

When you pray, pray for other people too.

Always find time to pray. Prayer is the best weapon you'll ever have.

Most of the time for us Humans, complaining about life is inevitable. But let's try to lessen it as much as possible.

Live life to the fullest, but in a right way. Take care of your life, you only have one.

It Doesn't matter how old you are, It's never too late to learn a new skill such as dancing or playing a musical instrument.

If you see an ambulance, say a little prayer for that person inside. They badly need it.

Being hurt is not an excuse for you to hurt other people.

Throw compliments to your partner every once in a while.

Never say compliments about other men/women to your partner. That's an insult.

Always share if you receive financial blessings. Become a blessing also to the people around you.

If you want to lose weight, either you eat right, or you don't eat anything at all for 16 to 20 hours a day. Believe me, I've done it.

Never forget and give back to that person who helped you during those times when everyone turned their backs on you.

Never be afraid to push yourself to the limit.

Wearing a new pair of shoes and an old pants looks better rather than wearing an old pair of shoes with a new pants.

If you're depressed, eat a piece of banana or a bar of chocolate. It helps.

If you're a busy person, 24 hours in a day is not enough.

Eating is good, but eating right is better.

A four hour continuous sleep is enough for an adult.

Falling in love and being loved back is the best feeling in the world.

Do not ever play with someone's feelings.

A kiss from the right person is way much better than having sex with the wrong one.

Humans suck at keeping promises.

People nowadays don't know what self-respect is.

We only see the value of our loved one once they're gone.

Humans apologize and do the same mistakes all over again.

Greed is one of the biggest factor of poverty.

Most of us only see the value of our health once we're ill.

Loyalty is rare, by any chance you find one, value and keep them.

Avoid an argument with your wife/girlfriend, most of the time you'll end up losing.

If you have extra money, feed those who are hungry.

Don't always depend on other people to give you help. Learn to stand up for yourself.

There will always be good looking and attractive people around you. If you can't say NO to temptations, you'd rather not put yourself into a relationship.

We fight and say hurtful things to our loved ones. By the time they are gone, you will forever regret every single hurtful words you've thrown at them. As much as possible, control your mouth and your emotions.

Save at least 2 months worth of your salary as an emergency fund.

A fight most of the time is never worth it, worst case if you can't avoid it, make sure you win it.

A loving heart is happier than a hateful heart.

You don't have to understand everything about your partner, if you really love them you just have to accept them.

Keeping a job is hard, but looking for a job is harder. Wherever you go there will always be shitty workmates. Learn to adapt and overcome.

Respect is Earned, it can't be bought.

Most people are alive, but not living life.

In life, you will experience pain and cause pain to other people with your journey of finding true Love.

If it's not worth it, don't do it.

Don't let your emotions control your judgment.

Nothing in this world is permanent. Stop wasting your time with negativity. Love fully, Love deeply. Love unconditionally. A life lived full of Love will attract positivity.

www.ingramcontent.com/pod-product-compliance
Lightning Source LLC
LaVergne TN
LVHW011728060526
838200LV00051B/3079